BINGSOP'S
FABLES

ALSO BY STANLEY BING

Biz Words

What Would Machiavelli Do?

Throwing the Elephant

Sun Tzu Was a Sissy

The Big Bing

Rome, Inc.

100 Bullshit Jobs . . . And How to Get Them

NOVELS

Lloyd: What Happened

You Look Nice Today

BINGSOP'S
FABLES

LITTLE MORALS FOR BIG BUSINESS

STANLEY BING

WITH ILLUSTRATIONS BY STEVE BRODNER

HARPER
BUSINESS

An Imprint of HarperCollins*Publishers*
www.harpercollins.com

HarperCollins books may be purchased for educational, business, or sales promotional use. For information, please write: Special Markets Department, HarperCollins Publishers, 10 East 53rd Street, New York, NY 10022.

FIRST EDITION

Designed by Renato Stanisic

Library of Congress Cataloging-in-Publication Data

Bing, Stanley.
    Bingsop's fables : little morals for big business / by Stanley Bing ; with illustrations by Steve Brodner.—1st ed.
       p.   cm.
    ISBN: 978-0-06-199852-2
    1. Organizational behavior—Moral and ethical aspects. 2. Management—Moral and ethical aspects. 3. Success in business—Moral and ethical aspects. 4. Corporate culture—Moral and ethical aspects. I. Title.
    HD58.7.B538   2011
    174'.4—dc22   2010051659

11 12 13 14 15   OV/RRD   10 9 8 7 6 5 4 3 2 1

To Laura

Either we must not speak to kings,
or we must say what pleases them.

—AESOP

CONTENTS

Translator's Note

People in business love instructional tales. Perhaps this is because we don't know what's going on and need assistance. And while we appreciate for this purpose a good anecdote or the occasional shaggy-dog tale, for wisdom and pith there is nothing as effective as the fable. That's because fables have a useful moral packed into every one, a little slogan to live by. That's good value for your dollar. Unlike the fairy tale, bloody saga, or juicy bit of gossip, a fable must educate while it amuses. For many a truth is spoken in jest.

Nowhere is this subtle blend of the sublime and the ridiculous more evident than in the charming fables laid down by the ancient scribe now known to the world as Bingsop. Long thought lost, these artifacts of an ancient corporate culture were discovered in an abandoned credenza tucked into the corner of a remote office whose tenant had gone Chapter 11 in some crash or other. Their provenance and importance were declared almost immediately by a host of Web destinations.

Of the man himself, we know little. He lived. He worked. He lunched. He got a few options. At the age of about thirty, as was customary of his time, he entered into formal servitude with a large corporation, taking an office in a far outpost of the enterprise with several fine museums but no nightlife. After a long period of enslavement, he received several excellent bonuses over a stretch of three or four years, and, thus purchasing his freedom, wandered off into underemployment. It is said he even became a consultant for a time, although to his credit such hearsay has never been verified.

Even in his indenture, Bingsop had it pretty easy. The corporations of that time rewarded the very high-level slave with a life of comfort and a certain amount of influence and power. Most important, Bingsop's functional position (which is not clearly defined in his writing) allowed him to travel as widely as the international tentacles of his company, studying the ways of human beings in a variety of business situations, from the most informal to the most structured and bizarre. New York, Rome, Tokyo, London, Paris, Los Angeles—he was known at respectable tables and hotels in every port. He spent time in the now submerged city that was once Miami. He worked with the great and the near great, most of whom are now lost in the shifting sands of time, although they certainly thought they were pretty big hotshots while it lasted. Unfortunately, not everyone was amused by Bingsop's act.

It was a miscalculated anecdote, in the end, that is thought to have laid him low. In the later part of his career, as he was touring about as an after-dinner speaker and juggler (capable of keeping three sheets of letterhead aloft without dropping or creasing a single one), he found himself in Las Vegas, talking to a phalanx of drunken security analysts and investment bankers. Finding them surprisingly dull of wit, and perhaps having drunk too much himself and having slept too little the night before, Bingsop neglected to disguise his message behind his customary veil of good humor, and the group, enraged at having paid a hefty sum for the pleasure of having an unflattering mirror held up to them, rushed the podium and beat him to death with the souvenir baseball bats they had received in their convention gift bags.

After this untimely end, the fame of Bingsop only grew, his fables moving across continents, speaking to generations of wage slaves and free executives alike with sagacity, subtlety, and charm. The truth is ever-evolving. It is the task of individuals like Bingsop to send that truth off into the world like a little child, where it may grow, gain force and definition over time, and perhaps one day change the world. Until that time, little tales such as these will always be welcome wherever they may go, particularly after dinner.

—STANLEY BING, JANUARY 2011

BINGSOP'S
FABLES

The CEO and his hatchet man planned
to execute their reorganization all at once,
on a Friday afternoon.

Shit Flows Downhill, but Not Forever

||||||||||||||||||||||||||||||||

After a horrible and bloody merger, the CEO of the losing side, who had barely survived the "coming together of two proud companies," did an analysis of which services could be outsourced in his conquered subsidiary. The CEO knew that his future depended on how many jobs he could kill before the size of his package was noted by the senior management of the dominant hedge fund that now owned them. He quickly saw that a number of internal functions could be managed offshore simply by hiring a service firm or existing entity in Costa Rica that did such things for companies looking to minimize pensions, benefits, and other employee-related costs. "I can save a ton of money and be a hero to my new bosses just like the guys at Citigroup did," he thought.

Like many CEOs, however, this particular executive, while a genuine fan of rationalizing costs, hated to actually fire people himself. He therefore determined to hire a hatchet man to do the nasty work for him, bringing in a former McKinsey operative and giving him the title of Chief Operating Officer. This COO was himself quite expensive, his salary, bonus, long-term compensation, and perquisites amounting to the cost of several hundred smaller jobs. He at once targeted Law, Accounting, Public Relations, Event Planning, Office Services, and several other formerly integrated departments for extreme unction, although he did spare the executive chef.

"This place is way fat," he told the CEO, who knew he was full of shit but admired the zeal with which he justified his compensation.

"This fellow is a real go-getter," said the CEO to himself. "I will kill him as soon as I can, for he is very dangerous to any life form in his vicinity."

The CEO and his hatchet man planned to execute their reorganization all at once, on a Friday afternoon, late in the day, when corporations traditionally "take out the garbage," minimizing as much as possible the media fallout.

On the day when the announcements were to be made, the Chief Operating Officer called the executives in charge of these various areas into his palatial office, one by one, and terminated them after outlining the actions necessary to earn their severance. And there was much weeping and gnashing of teeth throughout the building, which had once been home to several hundred worthy souls and would now be little more than a ghost town populated by wraiths whose jobs it would be to manage outsourced providers.

"These are tough times," said the COO to each of them. "And tough times call for hard solutions. Thank you for your contribution. Now get the fuck out of here." Actually, he didn't say that precisely. But that's precisely what he meant.

Among those called to judgment in this manner was a Strategic Planner who was the sole member of what had once been a functioning group of people hired to chart the long-term direction of the enterprise back when companies were less intent on operating strictly quarter to quarter. This planning dude was a savvy fellow, and had quietly functioned under the radar for quite some time. He earnestly beseeched the hatchet man to spare his life for the sake of superior operations.

"Dude," he said, adopting the modified surfer patois that binds together much of the more youthful cadre of senior management. "You can't take me out. This place is nothing without a planning operation that understands and is dedicated to the day to day. Give me a chance to exercise my chops and demonstrate my added value. Besides, I'm no lawyer. I'm no beancounter. I'm a Wharton grad, did six years at KPMG. I was instrumental in the transaction that produced this acquisition, for chrissake. At some point we're going to need to grow revenue, not just cut costs. That's when what I do really kicks in."

The Chief Operating Officer, who was a graduate of the Harvard Business School, laughed aloud and said, "It may be as you say, Fred. But if you were half as smart as you think you are, you'd have seen the personal implications of a merger like this one. I'm sorry, dude. You're toast."

Six months later, when the cutbacks were all done, the Chief Executive Officer fired this very same hatchet man with exactly the same words. "What a bastard," said the CEO to himself as he started the search for a new second banana, a search he didn't actually have time to complete before his new bosses at the hedge fund took *him* out, a step that cost them $147 million in severance but that they still considered a good investment. "What a bunch of losers," said the hedge fund officers. And then they had lunch.

MORAL: BIRDS OF A FEATHER DIE TOGETHER, ALBEIT WITH MUCH DIFFERENT EXIT PACKAGES.

Mini-Fable

THERE ARE MANY WAYS TO LOSE

An elderly Supply Chain Officer had hit his expiration date, and was hunkered down in his office. His colleagues came in great numbers to inquire after his health, and each one helped himself to a share of his turf, since he could no longer handle or protect it; so that in the end he was laid low not from the complications of his career malaise, but from the ostensible "help" he got from his friends. When he got fired, they all took him to Elaine's.

MORAL: EVIL COMPANIONS BRING MORE PAIN THAN PROFIT.

For the next six weeks, the Benefits Manager
listened only to hip-hop, becoming quite an aficionado
of sampling, backbeats, and slant rhymes.

The Human
Resources Guy
Who Became
Something of a
Hipster

||||||||||||||||||||||||||||

A Benefits Manager in the Human Resources Department of a rather gray and tedious insurance company had morphed into the human manifestation of his corporate culture. His suit was gray. His hair was gray. His tie was gray. Even his face, except for the hint of a day's beard shadow, was relatively gray. Only his shirt was white, although occasionally, when it was one of the older ones he had acquired quite some time ago, and had inadequately laundered, it too was a sort of gray. His socks were gray. His selection of art in his office, where the furniture was gray, was gray. At home, his cat was gray, as was his dinner. At the end of the year, his bonus was gray.

In spite of this preponderant lack of particular color, the Benefits Manager thought himself to be pretty happy, in a monochromatic sort of way. "This is life, or at least my version of it," he thought. "It is pointless to think otherwise. At least I help people receive the proper benefits that are due them, and prevent them from receiving those that are not. That is an important function in the operations of our company, and I am proud to provide it."

One day, a day much like the day before it, and the day before that, and the day before that, and the day that was likely to come, and the one after that, and so forth, the Benefits Manager of the corporation saw his Assistant on the plaza outside their building at noontime. She was listening to her iPod and moving to the music.

He knew her name was Christie, that she was twenty-three years of age, and entitled to ten days of salary if she were ever asked to leave the company, which was not contemplated, but always possible. He knew she had no dependents, took the lowest level of medical coverage, and had $87.43 in her 401(k). He could see the worst of any one of her terrible destinies. "Poor dear," he thought as he watched her dancing demurely to a song he could not hear. "She has so little, and it will be decades before she has amassed any true value in her package."

Mesmerized by the grace of her body while she danced, the Benefits Manager watched discreetly from a bench at the other end of the plaza. "My goodness," he said to himself. "She is quite beautiful. What is most stunning about her, in addition to her long auburn hair and tight, buoyant figure, is the obvious joy she feels in her sheer existence, and the pleasure that her selection of music has given her."

Suddenly a burst of golden light smote the Benefits Manager from above and he was seized by an insatiable desire to possess the same psychic and spiritual space within which his young Assistant danced. Approaching her politely, he reached his arm out of his gray penumbra and touched the radiant being on her shoulder.

"Excuse me, Christie," he said as she popped her earbud out of her auricular canal. "What are you listening to? I think I'd like to give it a try myself!" The truth was, he did in fact have a first-gen 20-gig iPod sitting somewhere in the depths of a kitchen drawer.

"It's a hip-hop mix, Bob," said the lithe and friendly support person. "If you want, I'll burn a CD for you."

"Would you, Christie?" he said, blushing to the roots of his hair, an unaccustomed redness that was not wholly uncomfortable. "That would be . . . the bomb."

For the next six weeks, the Benefits Manager listened only to hip-hop, becoming quite an aficionado of sampling, backbeats, and slant rhymes. He purchased a red tie and traded his wing tips for a pair of black Weejuns. Not long afterward, he died of a cerebral aneurysm.

MORAL: FISH GOTTA SWIM. BIRDS GOTTA FLY. KEEP IT STRAIGHT.

Mini-Fable

THE NEWBIE AND THE E-MAIL CHAIN

A Newbie who had just entered the corporation found himself embroiled in a project way over his head simply because he had been cc:'d on the e-mail chain. He ran to his senior officer and said, "I don't know how I got stung by this thing. I have a ton of work to do on it, and I was only cc:'d on the original." "That's why," his boss told him. "All the principals on the chain are out of it entirely, having delegated the work to those beneath them on the distribution. Next time, try fielding a strong response moving the ball to a different part of the field."

MORAL: SEIZE THE BULLSHIT BY THE HORNS.

The Limo Driver left the Mogul in the car,
hiked into town, and had a nice
dinner at the local tavern.

The Media

Mogul Who
Pissed Off
His Limo Driver

||||||||||||||||||||||||||||

One frosty day in late November, a Limo Driver was convey-ing a Media Mogul to a party given by Martha Stewart at her charming estate in rural Connecticut, where the drinks would be ice cold, the guest list steaming hot, and the roast beast cooked to perfection.

They were rocketing along a country lane where there was no cell phone service, propelled by the grouchy Mogul's con-stant, ill-tempered exhortations. "Faster!" yelled the Mogul, who was used to yelling at people he felt entitled to yell at. "I don't want to be late to this fucking thing!"

Coming upon a seriously marshy bend in the road, the Limo Driver lost control of his Lincoln Town Car stretch and the wheels of the ridiculous vehicle sank deep into a rut.

The driver, aghast at the prospect of being late to deliver his in-fantile, narcissistic charge to the infantile, narcissistic social event where he was expected, stood alone, looking at the automotive behemoth. After a while, when the master of all he surveyed did not emerge from the car to see what was going on or to assist in any way, the Limo Driver at last politely stuck his head into the warm, comfortable confines of the limousine and entreated his passenger to come and help him. "I'm sorry, Mr. Gobczek," said the Driver, "But it will go faster if we do this together."

The Mogul climbed out of the limo, assessed the situation, and thus addressed his conveyer: "Put a large stick under the rear wheels. Then gun the engine in a low gear. After that, if we're still in a rut and can't get out, I suggest you hike into town and arrange another limo for me and a tow truck for you. And from here on in, don't ask somebody else for help until you've done everything you can to help yourself."

The Limo Driver thought about this for a long moment, then said to himself, "Right," left the Mogul in the car, hiked into town, and had a nice dinner at the local tavern while the entitled captain of commerce sat in the car until it ran out of gas, heat, and light. He was rescued only by chance when a fellow Media Mogul, returning from the party, came upon him walking aimlessly down the lane in the middle of the night, cold, hungry, and even more convinced about the insufficien- cies of your average Limo Driver.

The second Media Mogul, recognizing the first as a loath- some competitor, picked him up anyway, so that he could have some leverage over him in subsequent business dealings. After they returned to Manhattan, the Good Samaritan also took the opportunity to provide the entire amusing story to Page Six.

MORAL: THERE IS A RIGHT AND WRONG TIME TO ANNOY OTHER PEOPLE.

Mini-Fable

THE CEO AND HIS MARKETING EXECUTIVE

A CEO about to set out for a cocktail party saw his Marketing Executive, on whom he depended for companionship and moderate sucking up, standing at the door stretching himself in the sun. The CEO asked him sharply: "Earl," he said. "Why do you stand there just gaping and scratching? Everything is ready but you, so come with me right away." The Marketing Executive, wagging his tail, replied: "Hey, Bob. I've been ready since four o'clock; it's me who's waiting for you." The CEO glared at him. "What the hell am I paying a guy six figures for?" he barked. "To do nothing but hang around here waiting for me?"

MORAL: BETTER LATE THAN FUNGIBLE.

"I don't know," said the Principal of the small start-up
to the Google Guy, who was drinking shots and
doing mail on his Android. "I liked being free."

A Google
Guy Shows
Why They're #1

|||||||||||||||||||||||||||||

APrincipal in a small start-up was sitting in his unpretentious office in one of San Jose's lesser boondocks, drinking a healthy Jamba Juice and working his butt off on the thing he loved, as usual. At approximately ten thirty a.m., he was visited by a Google Guy who was having his car repaired at the auto shop across the street. The Google Guy had been on his way to Sand Hill Road for a little scratch and sniff when his Prius started acting weird.

"I was just hanging out at the Piggly Wiggly and saw your logo," said the Google Guy to the Principal of the small start-up. "You guys do immersive games, right?"

Three hours later, the Google Guy's car was fixed but he was still there, performing the due diligence with a team of Googlers that had been deployed to a Marriott not far from the 101 just a couple of miles down the road.

At two a.m., the Principal in the small start-up sat in his conference room with the Google Guy, looking at the deal sheets. There was vodka on the table, and some caviar.

"I don't know," said the Principal of the small start-up to

the Google Guy, who was drinking shots and doing mail on his Android. "I liked being free. Doing whatever. What do you want with me, anyway? I'm little. I won't move your numbers a bit. Why don't you go after something that builds scale?"

"Look," said the Google Guy. "You're here. I'm here. I'd be crazy to let go of you. So let's do this thing. Then we can go out and have an excellent dinner with some dudes you're gonna love."

So that's what they did.

MORAL: RICH OR POOR, IT'S GOOD TO HAVE MONEY.

Mini-Fable

THE CLASH OF THE MICRO-TITANS

Two regional Vice Presidents were fiercely contending over mastery of their slab of the nation. One at last put the other to flight and gained control over the associated budget line. The vanquished Vice President skulked away and hid himself in his office in Dubuque, while the conqueror immediately moved his operation to Chicago and constructed an executive suite there fit for a pasha. He also gave a series of "strategic" dinners that were basically excuses to celebrate his accession to the regional throne. Eventually, he made so much organizational noise that he thoroughly aggravated the Chief Operating Officer, who was flying by for a sales meeting and noticed that nobody was paying him enough attention. The once-victorious VP was immediately banished to Omaha. This left the formerly vanquished as the most senior regional officer in good standing, and he at once rose to unparalleled power and influence, although he never did get out of Dubuque.

MORAL: PRIDE GOETH BEFORE DEFENESTRATION.

The Publishing Executive had compassion on the
Security Analyst and, putting her arm around the fellow,
took him into the restaurant and fed him a very good lunch.

Ugly
Lunch

||||||||||||||||||||||||||||||

O ne winter's day, a Publishing Executive, whose imprint was a visible part of a much larger global entertainment conglomerate, found a well-known Security Analyst who covered her industry standing outside of the Four Seasons restaurant in New York City, trying to cadge a free lunch and stay warm at the same time.

The Security Analyst, who had often played the role of guest in that establishment, was obviously in extremis. His nose was red and he was hopping up and down from one foot to the other in the classic dance that signifies desperate need of a men's room. The Publishing Executive had compassion on the Security Analyst and, putting her arm around the fellow, took him into the restaurant and—after that welcome visit to the restroom—fed him a very good lunch. In spite of the fact that he was there at the pleasure of his industry companion and the company behind her Platinum Card, the Security Analyst had no problem ordering a lobster appetizer, a nice slab of filet mignon, and a special soufflé for dessert. He also spent a significant amount of time perusing the wine list before selecting a pricey Cabernet, while his host, who had actual work to do in the afternoon, had the finest Bloomberg on the rocks. They spoke abstractly about interest rates and Sudoku.

After filling himself to the brim with wine and bonhomie, the Security Analyst permitted the Publishing Executive to tip the coat check, embraced his bosom friend at the front door, then went back to his midtown office and wrote a highly negative assessment of the enterprise that had just fed him expensively, inflicting a mortal wound on the expense account of his recent host, who was called to account by a variety of corporate watchdogs when her statement surfaced at the end of the month in Accounts Payable.

"Can I ask you why you were lunching with that scumbag?" her Chairman asked her in the elevator in a very not-nice tone of voice. And she truly did not know what to say. So she said nothing. "We have to keep an eye on that one," said the Chairman at his staff meeting later. "I don't like the company she keeps." They nodded.

MORAL: A $300 LUNCH SHOULD BE REPAID WITH KINDNESS.

Mini-Fable

THE INVESTMENT BANKER IN
CORPORATE CLOTHING

Once upon a time, an Investment Banker resolved to disguise his true, predatory nature and, in order to stay sleek in a dead market, joined a corporation as Executive Vice President (EVP) of something. Once at the heart of an established corporate structure, he found himself pastured with the senior management of the firm at all kinds of staff meetings, planning meetings, drink sessions, breakfasts, lunches, dinners, and boondoggles. After a while, he had everybody fooled, even the Chairman of the enterprise, who was a very careful and suspicious fellow most of the time. One day a deal appeared on the horizon that would make just a few of the big guys very rich, and screw the rest. So convincing was the Investment Banker in his new benign guise, however, that the Chairman didn't recognize him as a fellow sociopath, and took him out with all the others whom he considered sheep.

MORAL: NEVER COMPLETELY DISGUISE YOUR TRUE NATURE.

The Philanthropist took the masseuse to dinner
and for a romantic walk on the beach, and
found her to be a very good listener.

Just Because He's a Philanthropist Doesn't Mean He's Not a Dick

||||||||||||||||||||||||

A formerly horrendous billionaire-turned-warmhearted-philanthropist was getting a private massage in a little canvas enclosure close to the beach in Maui, when he took to rhapsodizing about the size and quality of his generosity to the young woman who at that moment was lathering his back with jojoba oil. His entourage waited outside, happy for the respite.

"I was once a really tough guy," he told the masseuse, his face buried in the little padded donut. "But now, I'll be honest with you, as God is my witness I don't think there's a guy with my kind of money who cares more about humanity . . . and animals."

The masseuse was an animal rights activist, and this impressed her. "Really?" she said. "That's awesome." And she went to work even harder on the big muscles of his upper legs.

"Ooh," said the philanthropist. "Absolutely." And, seeking to further impress her, he went on to talk about how much he loved all forms of life on the planet, even insects, and so on and so forth and blah blah blah, concluding, "I would not even swat a mosquito who landed on the bridge of my nose. I would just, you know, let it live."

"Wow," said the masseuse, "that is so nice."

This conversation was audible to the great philanthropist's Handler and the rest of his cadre, who were awaiting their boss's next spasm of need by passing the time playing cards in the hot sun outside the enclosure where he was having his body manipulated.

"Well, gentlemen," said the Handler, "it looks like we should all apply for the job of mosquito. They seem to have it better."

The young attendants, convulsed with the unexpected humor of the remark, lost control of their drinks and spilled a quantity of ice on the patio, at which point the great philanthropist came out of his cabana and sent them all into town, an eight-hour trip by Jeep over very bad roads, to get some very special sunscreen he had been wanting. While they were gone, he took the masseuse to dinner and for a romantic walk on the beach, and found her to be a very good listener.

MORAL: NEVER STAND BETWEEN A NARCISSIST AND HIS PLANS FOR THE EVENING.

Mini-Fable

THE HR GUY WHO CARRIED THE FLAG

A Human Resources guy hit the road to carry the corporate flag. Everywhere he went people prostrated themselves, knowing that the whole flag thing was the property of Bob, the iconoclastic CEO. The HR guy, however, got the notion into his head that the line employees were actually impressed with him, personally. This made him very proud, to the point where he began lingering in each location an extra day or two, and running up big expenses in the best restaurants and hotels. After about two months of this, he was recalled permanently to New York by the Chief Financial Officer, who kept an eye on his expense account for the duration of his contract.

MORAL: IT'S YOUR RING PEOPLE ARE KISSING, NOT YOU.

The Idiot Who Always Went Out Without a Coat, afraid that he would be discovered by his adversary to have changed his general stance on the subject of appropriate outer garb, went out in an open-collared shirt, all-season sport jacket, and light silk scarf.

What
Price Macho?

||||||||||||||||||||||||||||

The Idiot Who Always Went Out Without a Coat, no matter how severe the weather, bumped into the Ill-Tempered PR Person outside their Manhattan skyscraper on a moderately chilly afternoon in the early days of autumn.

The Idiot, as always, had just returned from an unpleasant search for some lunch, which he had undertaken in his shirt and tie, with no jacket, as usual, and certainly no topcoat. He was holding a small brown paper bag, whose contents were already beginning to harden in the cold. The Ill-Tempered PR Person was swaddled in a long Burberry trench coat, its flannel lining hard worn and its belt tightly cinched. A disposable but quite serviceable woolen street scarf encircled his ample neck.

"Well, you certainly look toasty," said the Idiot, dripping with sarcasm, presumably at the other's lack of masculine ability to withstand even a modest level of chill.

"Put on a coat, you moron," replied the other. Then they went their separate, jolly ways.

Several months went by, and a true winter descended

on them. One day at lunchtime each of them once again went out to brave the elements in search of food. The Ill-Tempered PR Person donned a tremendous cashmere overcoat, gloves, a first-rate silk-and-wool muffler, and a gigantic furry hat that made him look like a Soviet functionary, and walked a half block to the mandatory lunchroom of the day.

The Idiot Who Always Went Out Without a Coat, afraid that he would be discovered by his adversary to have changed his general stance on the subject of appropriate outer garb, went out in an open-collared shirt, all-season sport jacket, and light silk scarf. He was found several hours later in a snowdrift, frozen to death. His sartorial adversary was the first on the scene, and looked down with sadness upon the blue corpse.

"What an idiot," he said, but not without affection.

MORAL: EVEN FAIR-WEATHER FRIENDS SHOULD BE LISTENED TO.

Mini-Fable

THE MOGUL AND HIS SUPERMODELS

A middle-aged Mogul, whose hair had begun to turn rather sparse in inverse proportion to his girth, found himself pursuing two supermodels at the same time. One of them was obsessed with youth, which she was then on the point of losing, and the other was obsessed with food, which she was not permitted to eat. The latter got her vicarious thrills by making sure the Mogul ingested all sorts of delicacies and bonbons she would by no means permit herself. The former, terrified of the passage of years, was equally zealous in removing every gray hair she could find on his round little head. Thus it came to pass that between them he very soon found himself fat, bald, and alone.

MORAL: THOSE WHO SEEK TO PLEASE EVERYBODY PLEASE NOBODY.

Flat broke, empty of anything innovative or creative, the former Book Editor sat in a rented bungalow in West Hollywood, waiting for a meeting with a reality programming person from a minor cable network.

The
Ambitious
Book Editor and
the Super Agent

||||||||||||||||||||||||

The Ambitious Book Editor, oppressed by the deadlines others were failing to meet, was lazily basking at his desk in New York, enjoying the sunlight as it filtered through the hermetically sealed windows of his tower and imagining what would become of him if he didn't deliver on his obligations to populate the fall list.

His friend from Los Angeles, a Super Agent from a newly formed agency, was in town to suck up to a variety of clients and show his gray suit and slender tie to a variety of maître d's. Late that afternoon, this Super Agent, who had nothing better to do between a second lunch and an early drink, dropped by the Ambitious Book Editor's office, plopping himself down in the visitor's chair.

"Ah me," said the Book Editor to his friend, his voice heavy with sorrow, "I have so many great programming ideas, you know. But here I am chained to this boring job and this crummy desk."

The Super Agent, who knew a fair number of people who came from equally tedious occupations and had gone on to achieve some success in television programming, and sometimes even movies, listened sympathetically to his friend's lamentation. "I tell you what, Edgar," he said. "You give me fifteen percent of anything you come up with, and I'll get you aloft out there in no time."

Ecstatic, the Book Editor quit his day job and moved to the West Coast, where he set himself up in a manner that could bespeak success, rented a Bentley, and took a host of meetings with fatuous people who drained him dry of ideas and left him exactly nowhere, with no job, no capital, nothing. Worst, his friend the Super Agent was at a ten-day creative retreat where people discussed their vainglorious upcoming projects and had sex in Jacuzzis out of range of their wireless devices.

Flat broke, empty of anything innovative or creative, the former Book Editor sat in a rented bungalow in West Hollywood, waiting for a meeting with a reality programming person from a minor cable network. Reflecting on his career death, he exclaimed to nobody in particular (since nobody in particular was there), "I deserve what I have gotten! For what had I to do with thirty-second pitches, I who find it difficult to synopsize a novel in less than an hour?"

MORAL: FIFTEEN PERCENT OF VERY LITTLE IS NOT LIKELY TO HOLD CERTAIN PEOPLE'S INTEREST.

Mini-Fable

THE MICE AND THE CONSULTANTS

The Consultants and the Mice waged a perpetual war with each other, in which much blood was shed. The Consultants were always the victors. "That's because we're not organized and have no power hitters," said the Mice. They therefore appointed all their most august mouse leaders as their generals in the ongoing war, selecting only the most experienced, well-spoken, and best-looking among them. These new senior middle managers, having been invested with bogus titles that carried no pay implications, began dressing and comporting themselves as if they were true ultra-senior management. They had meetings. They wore $80 ties. They insisted on being seen only if somebody had an appointment. They issued memos. Upon the next round of reorganizational insanity, all the lower-level Mice immediately scampered off as fast as they could to their holes. The big Mice, conspicuous in their grandeur and weighted down with their sense of self-importance, were all captured and eaten by the Consultants.

MORAL: A LITTLE POWER IS A DANGEROUS THING.

The other Mogul replied: "Big deal. You own the guy
at *Fortune*. We have a friend at *Forbes*."

The Two
Publicity-Crazy
Moguls

|||||||||||||||||||||||||||||||

A couple of Media Mini-Moguls were sitting on a bench one fine summer morning. They were tolerant and polite to each other for a time, but soon they could stand such cordiality no longer, and each began to boast of the superiority of his business. This quickly devolved into an ongoing pissing contest that grew in intensity throughout the day. Then they got drunk and became fast friends. In the morning, they decided to rent a jet for the ride back to wherever.

On the plane back to their quotidian Mini-Mogul lives, they came upon a copy of a current issue of *Fortune*. It was sitting on the sideboard with the crudités and dip that were to precede their in-flight steak and salad. A stunning portrait of one of them grinning confidently was tucked under the cover's main banner, which read: "The Right Man at the Right Time?"

That Mini-Mogul, delighted by this development, said, "See? There you have it! I was meant to prevail over even a mighty and valuable enterprise such as yours." The other Mogul replied: "Big deal. You own the guy at *Fortune*. We have a friend at *Forbes*. We're on the cover there next week."

Then they both cracked up and secretly decided to kill their mogulish counterpart, which they eventually did, mutually strangling each other on CNBC *Power Lunch* one exceptionally slow news day.

MORAL: IF YOU THINK YOU'RE ONLY AS GOOD AS THIS WEEK'S PRESS, THEN YOU PROBABLY ARE.

Mini-Fable

THE SEMI-GENEROUS RECRUITER

A Recruiter for a Silicon Valley software company was attending a convention in Los Angeles. One evening, as the day's work was ending, there was a small earthquake that briefly shut down transportation in the area and stranded everybody in their hotels, with nothing to do but drink and mill about in the lobby. The recruiter took this as an opportunity to take a host of strangers to dinner, in hopes of luring them to his operation. The entire group of nearly a dozen repaired to the finest establishment in the hotel, while existing employees of the firm, on a very short leash, were dispatched to the snack bar in the lobby to fend for themselves on tuna fish and beer. The next day, everything returned to normal in LA, if there is such a thing, and all the Recruiter's new friends returned to their respective firms without even a good-bye. The Recruiter met up with one of them in an elevator and gave him a bit of a hard time. "I took care of you bozos and all I'm left with is a bunch of business cards," he said. "That's just it, man," said the fleeing programmer: "We got a pretty fair peek at how you treat your peeps once you reel them in."

MORAL: DON'T BE CHEESY WITH YOUR OLD FRIENDS WHILE IN PURSUIT OF YOUR NEW ONES.

So the Stupid Investor put his last $62,517 into the down market,
and that year he rebounded nicely in spite of the idiocy
of throwing good money after bad.

The Stupid

Investor Gets

Outsmarted . . .

Again!

||||||||||||||||||||||||||||||

The Stupid Investor, a great spendthrift, had run through all his patrimony and had but one good overcoat and a couple hundred grand left in liquid assets. One day he happened to see an Intelligent Hedge Fund Manager at one of those meaningless conferences held by research companies in a pretentious midtown hotel of moderate quality that smell of wet industrial carpet.

The Intelligent Hedge Fund Manager was twittering gaily about one digital start-up or another, and the Stupid Investor, supposing that a thaw in the tech market had begun, and knowing the Intelligent Hedge Fund Manager to be a lot smarter than he was, immediately invested the lion's share of his free cash in the venture.

Not many days later, the sector froze once again into a block of ice, and any chance the Investor had of recouping even a morsel of his cash without a long-term wait seemed remote indeed. On the bright side, the Intelligent Hedge Fund Manager too was rendered nearly illiquid and lost many of his clients, who had been whacked entirely.

One morning not long after, the Stupid Investor found the

bedraggled Intelligent Hedge Fund Manager sitting on the street with a sodden coffee cup in his hand and a vacant expression on his face. "You!" he said.

"Don't get up in my grill, Ned," said the Intelligent Hedge Fund Manager.

"I'm totally hosed by that thing," said the Investor. "All my assets are tied up in it and I have no free cash to bail myself out of the situation."

"Boo-hoo," said the Intelligent Hedge Fund Manager. "You knew what you were getting into. Besides, you only lost a hundred grand. Multiply that by a factor of ten thousand and you have some idea of what I lost for other people, including myself."

"I don't really give a fuck about you," said the Investor. "This is about me."

"Well," said the Intelligent Hedge Fund Manager. "A smart guy with another nut to offer could make a killing in this down market."

"Really?" said the Investor. "Tell me more."

So the Stupid Investor put his last $62,517 into the down market, and that year he rebounded nicely in spite of the idiocy of throwing good money after bad. For his part, the Intelligent Hedge Fund Manager played the same strategy and made $4 billion in personal income, which incidentally was taxed at a lower rate, thanks to capital gains regulations written by people just like him.

MORAL: IF YOU'RE STUPID, LISTEN TO SMART PEOPLE.

Mini-Fable

THE BLABBERING
MARKETING EXECUTIVE

A Marketing Executive was fond of pontificating about this, that, and the other to everybody he met. His boss, trying to turn excess of wind into an asset, assigned him to be the guy who made all the required speeches at all the conventions nobody wanted to attend. The Marketing Executive grew excessively proud of this role and went around bragging to one and all about his industry status, going so far as to appear on the cover of several trade magazines. One day, sporting his "Presenter" ribbon with pride on his lapel, he met up with a retired colleague who had nothing to do but attend such gatherings and was about to die from a surfeit of rubber chicken. "Why do you make such an exhibition of yourself?" said the crusty old dude. "That silly ribbon you wear is not, believe me, any order of merit, but on the contrary a mark of disgrace, a public notice to all men to avoid your professional bloviating." He then allowed the Marketing Executive to take him to dinner.

MORAL: NOTORIETY ISN'T FAME, BUT IT STILL PAYS FOR A LOT.

"This is only half!" said the guy, who then
took the $200 and beat him senseless.

Bob and Larry Have Some Trouble on the Road

||||||||||||||||||||||||||||||||

Bob and Larry were exiting the semifinals of a sporting event together late one Friday night in a tidy little midwestern city where a good steak could be had for under $20. It had been an exciting contest, which they had enjoyed from the corporate suite, and each had consumed between four and sixteen beers. The championship game, which neither planned to attend, was to be held the following Saturday. Neither had tickets for that event and hardly cared if it happened at all.

"I wonder if we could sell our tickets as souvenirs," said Larry, who had gotten $30 from some guy on an exit ramp at the last Super Bowl. Found money being perhaps the most exciting of all, he fondly recalled the thrill of getting a little something for an object that was worth absolutely nothing to him.

At that moment, a fat man in a tan bush jacket hove into view directly in their path. "Sell tickets?" he said. His eyes were glazed and it was clear that he was in the final stages of inebriation. Larry and Bob looked at each other. In their minds, which themselves were none too sharp, they each possessed a ticket worthy of sale, even though it had actually been used that night and was worthless to any but those interested in a souvenir of a semifinal that had been attended by some 85,000 people. "I got one," said Larry.

"How much?" asked the drunken fat man in the tan bush jacket.

"Two hundred bucks," said Larry, shooting for the moon.

"You got two?" said the bleary fellow, a tingle of greed invading his countenance.

"Yeah," said Larry. "But honestly, Bub, what do you want them for?" They were brokering dead paper, nothing more.

"My bidness," said the crafty ticket merchant.

"Well, okay!" said Larry and Bob as they looked on in disbelief. And the acquisitor, with great haste, as if he was the one getting over on his counterparts, forked $400 over to Larry, took their expired tickets, and scurried away.

THEY WALKED ALONG with the crowd for some distance in wonderment, each palpating his two $100 bills with disbelief and excitement. As they passed a group of rummies, one of them called out to the pair, "Tickets?" And Bob, still confused about how such a windfall had been achieved, stopped and asked, "Why would anybody want to pay good money for used tickets?"

"Used?" the guys said. "Nobody wants used tickets. We want tickets to next Saturday's game."

"Uh-oh," said Bob and Larry.

The two made their way in silence down the darkened street of the small Midwestern city far from their urban home. "You know, Bob," said Larry, "I think we just ripped off that drunk guy."

"We didn't mean to!" Bob remonstrated.

"Yeah, but," Larry replied.

"Give me your two hundred dollars back," said Bob. "I'm going to go look for the guy. I feel really bad."

"No, man," said Larry.

"Suit yourself," said Bob, and the two parted company, Bob plunging once more back into the churning, intoxicated crowd and Larry dragging himself back to the Hyatt, where he hoped to get lucky with Melanie Marcus from Special Events. Some five minutes later, Bob heard a great huffing and puffing behind him, and he turned to see the fat drunk in the tan bush jacket. "I suppose you think you're pretty smart," said the guy.

"No, no," said Bob. "I've been looking for you. Take back your money."

"This is only half!" said the guy, who then took the $200 and beat him senseless.

MORAL: NOT ONLY GOOD DEEDS GET PUNISHED.

Mini-Fable

THE GENERAL COUNSEL WHO LOST HIS FASTBALL

A CEO with a true love for acquisition and litigation held his General Counsel in the highest regard. Nobody was as important to him as long as there was a deal cooking or a nasty lawsuit in the works. After some time, however, even the most vicious operator needs to rest, and so it was with this CEO, who developed a love for fine wine and for sailing and even golf, and knocked off the Attila the Hun routine. As a consequence, the General Counsel, although still employed, grew as lazy and flabby as his master. He even started to look a bit like him, as dogs do. After a decade or so of this, the company once again found itself at war, this time against a hedge fund with nothing but ill intentions. A war council was immediately called, at which the CEO railed against the invading army and called for blood and fire to be brought down against them. After about an hour of this, the General Counsel fell into a light doze. Upon being rather rudely awakened, he said to his irate master, "You're gonna have to honcho this thing without me, Harry. You've had me doing nothing but real estate and employee contracts for the last six years. I can't turn back into a scumbag like you overnight."

MORAL: MOST VASECTOMIES CANNOT BE REVERSED.

Forgetting in his mindless delight that there was a transparent barrier between him and the nirvana he sought, he walked with full, lurching forward momentum into the clear plate-glass wall before him, breaking his face and knocking himself out completely.

The Very

Thirsty Young

Tech Guy

||||||||||||||||||||||||||||||

A Young Tech Guy, in New York to attend a trade show at the Javits Center, developed an unquenchable thirst that oppressed him from morning until night.

It began right after he checked into the Omni Berkshire on 52nd Street, a very nice hotel with well-appointed suites. As he dumped his fold-over bag onto a roomy lounge chair, his eye was drawn to the honor bar tastefully concealed in the living room's entertainment center.

Since his company was paying for his stay, and his job was to entertain potential investment suckers, he decided that the first sucker he would entertain was himself. Humming merrily under his breath, he opened the small refrigerator to find two of everything—two mini-bottles of Grey Goose, two Johnnie Walker Blacks, two Bombay Sapphires, two Becks, and so forth, a veritable Noah's ark of booze.

The next morning he awoke two hours late, and decided to blow off the convention center entirely and indulge in a little hair of the dog. To avoid embarrassment with his guys back in Mountain View, he kept up with his e-mail and made a number of cell calls from inaudible locations. And so it went for the next few days.

On the night before he was scheduled to depart, he went to meet a couple of bozos about something or other and, now very, very thirsty indeed, happened to pass an absolutely lovely bar, which was either on the corner of Central Park South and Sixth Avenue or possibly not. Before him, a thousand glowing bottles festooned the space just beyond the big front window, a huge bouquet of liquors beckoning—red, green, deep amber—in the nighttime glitter of the city street.

Entranced, suspended in time and space, the young, thirsty tech dude attained a state of high unconsciousness, ripe with joy and anticipation. Forgetting in his mindless delight that there was a transparent barrier between him and the nirvana he sought, he walked with full, lurching forward momentum into the clear plate-glass wall before him, breaking his face and knocking himself out completely. This comical sight was observed by a passerby, who snapped his picture with a cell phone and sold it to the *New York Post*, which ran it across two pages the next day, effectively ending his career in Silicon Valley, a business environment notoriously inhospitable to thirsty idiots.

MORAL: IT IS POSSIBLE TO HAVE TOO MUCH FUN.

Mini-Fable

THE PURCHASING DEPARTMENT PROVES IT'S NO DUMMY

A Consultant, hearing that the Purchasing Department of a certain corporation was having workflow issues during a transition to a new online database system, did himself up in his best pinstripe and, taking his laptop, laser pointer, and stack of PowerPoint presentations in hard copy, went to call on their department head. He knocked at the door and inquired of the inmates "Whassup?" adding that if they needed help maximizing efficiency and so on and so forth, he would be happy to give them some advice. They replied, "We are all very well, and will continue to be so, if you will only be good enough to go away and leave us alone."

MORAL: SOME CURES ARE WORSE THAN THE DISEASE.

The Hedge Fund Manager then headed off to a small,
remote villa two hours south of Puerto Vallarta.

Dude! Where's My Money?

||||||||||||||||||||||||||||||

A Hedge Fund Manager by the improbable but appropriate name of Wiesel one day fell into a deep well of debt and could find no means of escape. "Woe is me!" he cried out to himself, for there was no one else around to listen. "I am lost! For there is certainly no one credulous and foolish enough to listen to my advice at this stage of the global economic melt-down, and I have no friends left to bilk!"

Fortunately for him, however, there was in fact one investor whose greed still outstripped his better judgment, a naive investor by the unlikely but fitting name of Seagul. Seduced by the memory of quick triple-digit returns once offered to the dumb and daring, this Seagul saw the Hedge Fund Manager at lunch one afternoon and, regarding his $5,000 pinstripe suit and $200 plate of salmon and greens, inquired if business was exceedingly good again. "You look terrific, Mort," he said to the Hedge Fund Manager, who was at that moment considering which variety of suicide might be the most painless.

Concealing his sad plight under a merry guise, Wiesel indulged in lavish praise of the business climate, exclaiming how it was excellent beyond measure, and encouraged Seagul to jump in on several key strategic moves that he was planning to accomplish that very day.

"I'll have to think about it," said the credulous investor, adopting a thoughtful and judicious mien, much as a goose may appear simultaneously dignified and utterly stupid.

"Dude," said the speculator. "Time is the one thing a deal like this cannot abide." He then mesmerized the other with a bale of economic mumbo jumbo about the frailty of exchange rates and the potential upside and downside implications of inaction.

So, mindful only of his greed, and without appropriate consultation with his financial advisors or even his wife, Seagul thoughtlessly jumped into the proposed commitment, which had something to do with the differential between the value of euros and Swiss francs.

As soon as the wire had cleared, however, the Hedge Fund Manager took the credulous investor to a local watering hole, bought him a double scotch, and informed him of the perils surrounding them, quickly suggesting a scheme for their common escape. "Dude," said he, "your money is now just keeping us afloat for the next forty-eight hours or so, but if you would kick in another large investment right now, we might just stand a chance of leveraging that chunk of cash into a new position in barley. If it's timed correctly, it could vault the both of us into the stratosphere in a matter of hours!" The credulous investor drank his double Glenlivet and assessed the matter. "And if you do not," said the Hedge Fund Manager, "we've both screwed the pooch."

"Okay, Mort," said the investor, who was not really an investor at all but a gambler in a casino with rules he couldn't possibly understand because there weren't any.

The Hedge Fund Manager immediately used the now prodigious size of the other man's wager to dig himself out of the hole he was in, then headed off to a small, remote villa two hours south of Puerto Vallarta. As he was headed across the border for a nice long stay, he received one last call over his smartphone, which was state-of-the-art and did just about everything but tweak his gonads. It was, of course, Seagul.

"Mort!" he cried over the very scratchy connection. "How could you do this to me?" To which the Hedge Fund Manager replied, "Dude, if your brain wasn't in your pecker, you'd have never gone into a thing like this without mapping a way out. I don't feel one bit guilty about this, because I'm a psychopath. What's your excuse?" And he hung up. Two weeks later, he was offered a prestigious senior role in a local drug cartel, which he immediately accepted.

MORAL: WATCH OUT FOR PEOPLE WHO CALL YOU "DUDE" WHEN THERE'S MONEY ON THE TABLE.

Mini-Fable

THE CONTROLLER WHO CRIED INVESTMENT BANKER

A Controller in the corporate headquarters of a large conglomerate was in charge of watching market activity on their stock. After the current recession, the value of that security had been reduced by some 120 percent, and the firm was trading at far less than its former market cap. Four or five times in six months, the Controller, basically to amuse himself, called a general alarm via e-mail, and even, once, a large staff meeting at which he freaked everybody out by crying "Investment Banker!" and citing a bunch of metrics nobody understood. Each time this occurred, the Controller would chuckle afterward about the delicate nerves of senior management. One day the dark event came at last and a run was made on their voting shares by Citadel, a horrible hedge fund that eats jobs for lunch. The Controller, now really alarmed, sent a global e-mail to all his bosses, all in CAPS, shouting for help, but no one paid any heed to his cries, nor rendered any assistance. The first ones eliminated in the subsequent takeover were the in-house Controllers.

MORAL: THERE'S NO SUCH THING AS "TOO PARANOID" ANYMORE.

"Accountant?" said the Accountant. "What makes you think I'm an Accountant?" And he pointed to his pocket protector.

The Karma
Chameleon CPA

||||||||||||||||||||||||||||||

An Accountant who had survived six mergers, two stupid acquisitions, and at least a dozen horrendous reorganizations was taking a five-minute respite from performing duties formerly assigned to sixteen of his now departed peers, and having a drink of water at the last remaining watercooler in the building (the rest having been taken away by cost containment experts).

Unfortunately for him, this disgraceful indolence was noticed by a Management Consultant who had been hired to hack still more limbs from the already seriously truncated corpse of the corporate body.

"Look," said the Consultant to himself. "There's a person getting a drink of water. He's obviously underutilized." And he made a note.

Having been through so much for so long, however, the CPA noticed the Consultant noticing him and, more important, noted the note that was being taken. He decided to confront the perilous situation directly.

"I know I've been caught in the act of being insufficiently

productive at this particular moment," he said to the Consultant, who was pretending to be a potted plant. "But I am a very hardworking person and I would like you to overlook this small indiscretion."

"I'm afraid not," said the Consultant, who was feeling extremely peckish, having just read a profile in *Barron's* of his Wharton roommate, who was now apparently helping children in the Dominican Republic receive proper dental care. "Look, what is your name? Larry? Larry, you have a job. I have a job. And in case you didn't know, while Finance is supposed to be the front line in efficiency, there are no fewer than two hundred accountants working for this corporation right now. And here I see you sort of, you know, jerking off? What am I supposed to think?"

"Accountant?" said the Accountant. "What makes you think I'm an Accountant?" And he pointed to his pocket protector.

"Well, I dunno," said the Consultant, now confused. "You're here in the butt end of the Finance floor. What am I supposed to think?"

"Well," said the Accountant. "I'm not an Accountant. I'm sort of insulted that you think so. I'm Tech Support, obviously."

"Well, okay, then," said the Consultant, who was deeply uncomfortable with the length and depth of this human interaction. "Sorry I bothered you." Then he went back to his temporary office and Googled a bunch of shit for a while.

"I'm taking a little walk," he said to this Consultant, who was by all measure precisely the same as the previous Consultant, something that seems to happen to people when they go to Consulting school. "I hope you won't hold this against me."

This Consultant looked at the pocket protector the Accountant was now wearing as a matter of course, and then informed him that he had a very special hostility reserved for Tech Support people, who he felt had taken over the entire twenty-third floor like a plague of mice.

The Accountant then assured the Consultant that in no way was he a member of Tech Support. In fact, he was just a hard-working Accountant, and even went so far as to take him to his tiny warren and demonstrate his aptitude with a desk calculator.

"Hm," said the second Consultant, who was late for something outside the office. "I'm just looking for Tech." And then he went away.

And thus our clever Accountant a second time escaped.

MORAL: DO WHAT YOU GOTTA DO. PERIOD.

Mini-Fable

HOW THE SLEAZY WALL STREET CROOK GOT THAT WAY

A boy stole a test from the older brother of his friend and used it to get an A in English, a subject for which he had no natural ability. He bragged about it to his mother, who approved of everything he did, even the bad stuff. Sure enough, she not only abstained from beating him, but encouraged him. Next time he stole a lovely handbag from Bloomingdale's and brought it to her, and she again commended him. The young man grew to adulthood, and was employed by every scamming firm that worked the edges of the financial industry, until he developed his own Ponzi scheme that ended up bilking several hundred million dollars from unsuspecting people of his own faith. As he was being led away to a comfortable life in a celebrity prison, he gave one final interview to Larry King. "I'll tell you the truth, Larry," he said, looking thoughtful and abashed. "If my mother had beaten me the first time I stole a pack of gum, I wouldn't be in this position now." Even Larry King thought he was full of shit, and that's saying a lot.

MORAL: IT'S WAY TOO EASY TO BLAME YOUR MOTHER,

AND, FRANKLY, NOBODY CARES.

After the vicious carnivores were gone from the Board Room, the Grunt entered the large and well-appointed space and, quite delighted, exclaimed to his vast superior, "Okay! You made fun of me when I said I could help you. But here we are!" And then he stood there, beaming.

The
Executive

Vice President
of Whatever and
the Tiny Grunt

||||||||||||||||||||||||||

The Executive Vice President of something indescribable was awakened in his opulent lair from a perfectly good nap by a Tiny Grunt who had been called to his office to put new batteries into his mouse.

Normally, this would have been okay, but the Grunt had entered without knocking. It was noontime, and he had been informed that the EVP would be out lunching.

Instead, he witnessed the snoozing executive facedown on his couch, drooling into the upholstery. He had, in short, seen that which must never been seen. Medusa's head. The destruction of Sodom. His fate was sealed before his very eyes.

Rising up angrily, the grouchy executive seized the young fellow by the shirtfront and yammered blearily into his face for a while, finally releasing him with a promise to refer his name to someone dire in HR. The Grunt, who needed to hold the job for another six months for it to have any value at all on his résumé, piteously entreated the flatulent nabob, saying: "If you would only spare my life, I would be sure to repay your kindness."

The Executive Vice President roared with laughter. It tickled him, the idea that a teeny-weeny grunt of this infinitesimal size could help Him. "As if!" he said. Then he let him go and forgot the whole thing. And life went on as normal, with all naps being taken and batteries being replaced at the appropriate times.

It happened shortly after this that the Executive Vice President of Whatever was trapped in a lengthy presentation with a group of predatory Controllers, who had caught him in several internal contradictions about a recently completed acquisition and were about to skin him alive. The Tiny Grunt was watching from the A/V control room, saw his discomfort, and cut the power to the video conferencing system, which of course ended the meeting. "He can get his shit together on his own time and come back later," said the Grunt, who had absolutely no reason to help the Executive Vice President of Whatever. For some reason, simple folk are often far kinder and more considerate than their more elevated counterparts.

After the vicious carnivores were gone from the Board Room, the Grunt entered the large and well-appointed space and, quite delighted, exclaimed to his vast superior, "Okay! You made fun of me when I said I could help you. But here we are!" And then he stood there, beaming.

"Yeah. Thanks," said the recipient of the favor somewhat graciously. At the same time, he made a mental note to wreak revenge on the little creature later for having made him slightly vulnerable. "Who does he think he is?" he thought. "Little pisher."

MORAL: YOU CAN HELP THE BIG GUYS. BUT THEY APPRECIATE IT DIFFERENTLY.

Mini-Fable

THE TWO DOGS OF CHAIRMAN MAL

Chairman Mal had two dogs: a hard-hitting sales hound who was on the road 350 days a year and a well-trained spaniel who kept him company back at their gigantic office tower in New York. When he returned home after a successful trip to the field, Chairman Mal and his trusty spaniel would invariably spend long evenings drinking, talking, and sampling the best food that the greatest city in the world had to offer. The loyal spaniel also earned perhaps ten times what his counterpart did, pulling down well into seven figures. This quite naturally annoyed the hound, who bitched to his pal at headquarters, "I don't get it. I work my ass off to produce revenue and you don't do shit here but sit around in meetings and look out the window, and you make a pile while I'm still on commission." The house dog replied, "Don't blame me, Bob. Blame Mal. He wrote our job descriptions."

MORAL: HATE THE GAME. NOT THE PLAYER.

"Let me put it to you another way," he said to Warren, who was
his favorite. "If you continue to fight with Harry
and Larry and Biff and Ilene, I will make your life a living Hell."

The End

of the

Enlightened

Manager

||||||||||||||||||||||||||||||

A very excellent Department Head had a close-knit cadre of hardworking subordinates who were perpetually quarreling among themselves. After a while, this really started to get on his nerves. He called one of them in.

"Warren," he said to his rather well-intentioned subordinate. "Why can't you get along with Harry, Larry, Biff, and Ilene?"

"They don't respect my function," said Warren, who in fact walked around all the time with a huge wad of resentment toward his peers clogging his guts, and was not aware of any need to moderate it.

"I assure you they do!" said the Department Head, but he was very weary. He then called in the others, one at a time.

"Why can't you guys get along with each other?" he asked them, one and all, and received in reply a different whinge from each about this and that or the other thing.

Finally, thoroughly sick of having to deal with all the interpersonal problems in his department, he called each in again.

"Let me put it to you another way," he said to Warren, who

was his favorite because he was very hardworking and never brought him a problem he had not already solved, at least conceptually. "If you continue to fight with Harry and Larry and Biff and Ilene, I will make your life a living Hell. I will never promote you. I will interrupt your vacations. I will fail to sign off on your expenses for months on end. I'm sick of arguing and cajoling and being reasonable. Get along. Or get out of here." Then he kicked Warren out of his office.

He then repeated this little speech to each and every one of his reportees, who listened very carefully and left terrified of their boss, having seen a side of him they had never experienced before. So instead of simple love and respect binding them to their senior officer, there was a new dimension to their reporting relationship.

Fear.

And from that time forth, all the children got along.

MORAL: EMPLOYEES CAN BE REALLY FUCKING TIRESOME IF YOU DON'T TELL THEM WHAT YOU WANT VERY, VERY CLEARLY.

Mini-Fable

THE BIG AND EVEN BIGGER AGENT

A really scary Big Agent who ran a fair chunk of the TV business in LA entered into a partnership with an even scarier, Even Bigger Agent to more easily capture the lion's share of the talent market that season. "I'm faster than you are," said the Big Agent to the Even Bigger Agent, "but you are a lot larger and stronger. Between us we'll be unbeatable." Then they each had a big laugh (possibly for different reasons, it turns out) and an even bigger martini, even though it was only noon. Several months later, when the development season had ended, their combined market share was obscene. At that point, they got together and the Even Bigger Agent divided their spoils into three shares. "Why three?" asked the Big Agent, suddenly feeling rather nervous. "Well, Biff," said the Even Bigger Agent, "I'll take the first share, because, honestly, without my leverage we wouldn't have dick, and I will also take the second share, and you know what, believe me, the third share will just be a source of great evil to you unless you basically just fork it over and get out of here before I decide to completely fuck you over in this town, which you know I can do." Then he went off to an evening honoring him as a great philanthropist.

MORAL: MIGHT MAKES RIGHT, PARTICULARLY IN CERTAIN COMMUNITIES.

At the snack session, a small manager in the Special Events
unit of the corporation was asked by an ultra-senior officer
what she thought of the new, more democratic order.

Some Are More Equal Than Others

|||||||||||||||||||||||||||||||||

The Happy Employees in the cities, towns, and outlying locations of the Company had a benevolent Chairman as their beloved leader. Bob was good-natured, tyrannical within tolerable limits, almost never cruel, in general as gentle and tender a Chairman as can be expected (except perhaps when his morning muffin was even the slightest bit stale). In the tenth year of his tenure, he read a business book on Vision and how important it was to have one, preferably expressed in a Vision Statement.

"I have never had a Vision Statement," he said to himself, and felt very sad. Then he brightened. "But I can get one!" And then he got busy. He immediately sent out a company-wide memo inviting all those of manager title and above to attend a boondoggle at Sanibel Island on the west coast of Florida, at a lovely resort featuring sand and surf, great food, golf, and plenty of sunshine.

At that historic gathering, which was attended by more than five hundred managers, directors, vice presidents, executive vice presidents, senior executive vice presidents, and presidents, of which there were many, as well as the chief financial officer, chief communications officer, chief operating officer, and the Chairman himself, a Vision Statement was developed and all departments took a pledge of Teamwork and Equality for the Good of All, a pact under which the executives and middle management of Investor Relations, Corporate Communications, Finance, Marketing, Operations, Management Information, Human Resources, New Media, and all other departments promised to live together in peace, amity, and mutual respect, regardless of rank or title.

"Now we are all one!" he said to the packed ballroom, and everybody cheered and broke for Danish.

At the snack session, a small manager in the Special Events unit of the corporation was asked by an ultra-senior officer what she thought of the new, more democratic order. The young woman looked deeply into the eyes of the powerful executive, thought for a moment, then said, "Oh, how I have longed to see this day, in which the weak shall take their place with impunity by the side of the strong." After she said this, she took a scant look at the group around her, quickly fled the building, and took the first plane back to St. Louis.

MORAL: WHEN THE LION LIES DOWN WITH THE LAMB, ONLY ONE OF THEM SHOULD SLEEP WITH BOTH EYES CLOSED.

Mini-Fable

HOW TO SCARE A BLOGGER

A Blogger was searching for rumors about a certain Mogul who had become a designated target in the digital space. The Blogger asked an Industry Analyst with whom he was having lunch if he had heard anything damaging or invidious about the Mogul in question, or stories of uncertain provenance about those near and dear to him. The Analyst, who was relatively well connected, said to the Blogger, "Actually, I'm somewhat friendly with the guy you're talking about. If you want to meet him I can arrange it." The Blogger, turning very pale, teeth chattering, replied, "No, thanks! It's just rumors I'm looking for, not the guy himself."

MORAL: A LARGE NUMBER OF BLOGGERS WELL AND TRULY SUCK.

On his own birthday, he received a huge number of useless
but well-intentioned gifts from his clients, upon
which he said to himself, "Go figure."

The Sales

Guy Who Was Obsessed with People's Birthdays

||||||||||||||||||||||||||||||||||

A Sales Guy named Leonard Popnick was a big believer in remembering the birthdays of his customers. He swore by it. His BlackBerry pinged him several days before the birthday of each and every one of his clients. He would then buy a nice pen, scarf, or cute mechanical toy, and send it off to them with an affectionate note just in time. This resulted in virtually no sales, although he did receive some nice thank-you cards and became something of a legend in his business. People spoke to each other of having been "popnicked," and they laughed a bit, though not unkindly.

At last, having pursued this practice for several years and noting its general ineffectiveness, the Sales Guy determined to get out of his office, go to each client's headquarters, pitch them in person, take them to the best steak place in town, and chew on their leg until they agreed to sign on the dotted line. This produced a large number of sales and made him the Sales Professional of the Year for his corporation.

On his own birthday, he received a huge number of useless but well-intentioned gifts from his clients, upon which he said to himself, "Go figure."

MORAL: THE DIRECT APPROACH IS OFTEN BEST IF YOU'RE SELL-ING SOMETHING.

Mini-Fable

THE M&A LAWYER AND HIS SHADOW

Early one morning after an all-night session with his counterpart in the target company, a drunken Mergers and Acquisitions Lawyer was crossing a footbridge over a man-made pond with some deal papers in his mouth. Delirious with exhaustion and greed over the personal implications of the deal to his financial profile, he saw his own shadow in the water and took it for that of another M&A lawyer with a deal twice the value of the one he was working on. He immediately let go of his own papers and fiercely attacked the image of what he believed to be the other M&A guy in the reflecting pool. He thus lost both: that which he grasped at in the water, because it was a shadow; and his own, because while he wasn't looking, a guy from another investment bank snatched it up and ran away with it.

MORAL: GREED CAN BE A BAD STRATEGY, EVEN WHEN THEY PAY
YOU FOR IT.

"Come on, Andy," said the PR executive to the Bald Little Beancounter, drooling over the prospect of all that money being booked and none of it plowed back into his operating group. "There's millions here."

The Bald
Little Beancounter
Keeps
His Beans Dry

||||||||||||||||||||||||||||||||||

Bald Little Beancounter was burning the midnight oil one late December evening at the end of the fourth quarter, counting all the beans collected by the Accounts Receivable Department during the fiscal year.

"How well we all have done!" he said to himself, and danced a merry Beancounter dance, without actually moving. This Lenten entertainment was interrupted by the head of Public Relations, who had heard the jollity and wandered in from his depopulated corner of the floor.

"Come on, Andy," said the PR executive to the Bald Little Beancounter, drooling over the prospect of all that money being booked and none of it plowed back into his operating group. "There's millions here. Can't you spare a few crumbs for what the Chairman recently called 'the most important part of our public positioning effort'? I'm dying here. I'm having to print our press clips on both sides of the page. We're reusing coffee cups. My people can't order appetizers at lunch."

The Beancounter laughed his jocose beancounter laugh, while still looking stern and offended, then inquired of him,

"Randy. Why did you not build in false expenses to cushion your operating expense line at last year's budget time? And having not done so, why did you spend what little you had like a drunken sailor taking totally extraneous people to dinner all year round and going to Vegas last summer for a completely extraneous convention that sensible people avoided entirely?"

The PR executive sighed and replied, "I didn't think about it. We always go to that convention. Old habits die hard, I guess."

"Fine," said the Beancounter tartly. "You had fun all summer. Now you'll have to suck it up in the winter."

MORAL: NEXT TIME YOU GO TO VEGAS, MAKE SURE TO INVITE FINANCE TO THE PARTY. THEY GENERALLY APPROVE THEIR OWN EXPENSES.

Mini-Fable

THE MAGAZINE EDITOR AND HER POOR #2

A Magazine Editor had one solitary person reporting to her, an individual named Esme who had begun as her assistant but was now, due to the collapse of that industry, assigned to so many tasks that nothing was done very well anymore. At the time each week when the magazine was scheduled to be published, the Editor would load the poor #2 down with everything imaginable, and was herself so overburdened that she was screwing up all over the place as well. Consequently, the magazine, which had for a time been quite respectable, now pleased no one, and was as thin as the young women pictured in its Summer Fun issue. Finally, Esme could stand it no longer, and said to her frazzled boss, "Midge, what good does it do to squeeze every last drop of blood out of us both? If you're looking to land us both in a psych ward, you're doing a great job. If you're trying to put out a magazine, we need to hire another assistant and make HER life miserable." And that's what they did.

MORAL: YOU DON'T GET WHAT YOU DON'T PAY FOR.

Terrified at the sight of the two pin-striped beasts about to
feed on yet another helping of flesh, he lifted his eyes and
his hands to heaven, and vowed to eat peanut butter and jelly
for three months if he might only secure his escape.

The Head
Who Lost His
Headcount

|||||||||||||||||||||||||||||||

A Department Head tending his business at a very difficult time of the year went through a zero-based budgeting process and lost some key bodies from his headcount. After a long and fruitless attempt to protect them, he was informed by a rather cold memo from Human Resources of the steps that had been taken. Saddened and enraged not only at the human cost but at the implications for the productivity of his operation, he made a vow that, when he discovered the unknown enemy in the ranks of ultra-senior management who had authorized the debilitating staff cuts, he would throw a huge dinner at Balthazar for the survivors with his excess budget at year end. So swashbuckling did he feel after this statement that he almost worked himself up into a decent mood.

Not long afterward, as he was having a quiet lunch in one of the executive dining rooms on the egregiously opulent fortieth floor of his tower, he happened to see a suit from McKinsey in the small conference room with the Chairman, closely scrutinizing a large spreadsheet filled with names. He was pretty sure his name was on it, and even if it wasn't, he felt the cold hand of professional mortality on the back of his neck.

Terrified at the sight of the two pin-striped beasts about to feed on yet another helping of flesh, he lifted his eyes and his hands to heaven, and said: "Just now I vowed to blow off my excess capital at a big seafood extravaganza if I could only find out who was responsible for the senseless pillaging of my head-count; but now that I have discovered how close I personally am to the abyss, I would willingly eat peanut butter and jelly at my desk for three months if I may only secure my own escape from these heartless beasts in safety!"

Then he went into the conference room, his heart in his mouth, and worked with the two predators to minimize the carnage as much as he could. After he was gone, the two looked at each other. Then the Chairman said, "You know, Don isn't a bad guy. He knows the drill. Take his name off the list."

MORAL: TO SUCCEED, ONE MUST FIRST SURVIVE.

Mini-Fable

TWO CAPTAINS OF INDUSTRY FIGHT OVER A TABLE

On a particularly busy Wednesday, when a leading blog tracked who got the best table at Michael's restaurant in Manhattan, two CEOs in $3,000 suits (not to mention $650 Brioni shirts) appeared at the reception area at precisely the same moment. As sometimes happens, they had been assigned to the same table, and one would have to surrender his position and take a slightly lesser spot. They immediately fell to disputation and would have clawed each other's faces off if Steve, the maître d', had not stood between them. When they stopped suddenly to catch their breath for a fiercer renewal of the fight, however, they saw a line had formed behind them made up primarily of journalists, who were closely observing their inane behavior. At that point each immediately fell over the other to surrender his position in a great show of largesse. They ended up embracing with great warmth before heading off to their assigned tables, which were, in fact, next to each other.

MORAL: OBSERVATION CHANGES THE NATURE OF THAT WHICH IS OBSERVED.

"Let the best man win," said the Guru, who believed the
hair up his ass was one of his greatest assets.

The Finance

Guy and the
Digital Guru with
a Wild Hair
Up His Ass

||||||||||||||||||||||||||||||

The Digital Guru with a Wild Hair Up His Ass one day ridiculed the rather deliberate attention span and process-based approach of the Finance Guy in regard to a certain large transaction their enterprise was undertaking. The latter replied, laughing: "You may be fast, but I'll get to the finish line of this thing before you do." The Guru, believing this assertion to be simply impossible, said, "Sure. Bring it on." They agreed that the Company's General Counsel should issue a deal memo with points that needed to be resolved by negotiation with all parties, internal and external, and fix the time and place of the final meeting with senior management, where the deal was to be evaluated and either approved or rejected. "Let the best man win," said the Guru, who believed the hair up his ass was one of his greatest assets.

On the day appointed, the two rose bright and early. In fact, the Guru had been working desperately through the night, attempting to construct rational models where before he had none, having been content simply to wow the multitudes with a lot of fast and flashy chatter. In the hours before the big meeting, he downed cup after cup of espresso, which he drew from a special machine he had installed in his office, and produced a blizzard of confusing paper even he did not fully understand.

For his part, the Finance Guy arrived at his normal hour with some coffee in a paper cup with pictures of the Parthenon on it. He had a raft of neat documentation that had been prepared in his usual tedious manner, showing how the purpose of the negotiations could be achieved in an entirely different and less spectacular way over a long period of time, a process that would require a great deal of effort and no dramatic results in the short term. His financial models, based on conservative assumptions, were impeccable from top to bottom line, and eminently defensible.

The ultimate meeting began and all were there but the Guru, who had fallen asleep at his desk, exhausted from the physical cost of the protracted attention to detail that had been required of him. At last, he arrived at the boardroom to find the meeting over and the Controller sitting by himself in the quiet of the gigantic and well-appointed space, eating a tuna fish sandwich and savoring his supposed victory. The Digital Guru with a Wild Hair Up His Ass then went in to see the CEO, scared him with a bunch of fantastical scenarios, and killed the deal entirely. The following week he left for a big job at Facebook.

MORAL: SLOW BUT STEADY WINS THIS PARTICULAR ITERATION OF THE RACE.

A vice president of Human Resources overheard their lamentations
in an area populated by company people of all ages,
many young and impressionable.

The Hopeful
Employees and
the Cash Balance
Pension Plan

||||||||||||||||||||||||||

A bunch of Hopeful Employees, sitting in the lunchroom of their corporate headquarters, were perusing material circulated by the Human Resources Department about the new "cash balance" pension plan that had replaced the one previously in place, which guaranteed a quantifiable payout at retirement for longtime workers. The new plan was stock-based, and the printed material showed impressive bar graphs demonstrating how much each pension would be worth at retirement age, assuming the company's stock grew at the Dow Jones average each year for ten, twenty, and thirty years.

When several years had passed, these same Employees sat once again with their tuna melts and looked at material describing how their pensions were doing. They perceived that the bar graphs had altered somewhat, and that the promised payout at retirement was less impressive than it had been with their prior pension. "We'll still do all right," they said to each other.

Time passed, and the group, each of whom was now quite elderly, once again gathered over individual pan pizzas and scrutinized the glossy report on how their pensions were faring. The bar graphs now showed that anyone who retired in the next several years would barely be able to afford life in a small rented recreational vehicle, although new, young workers were most certainly assured a fantastic windfall when they themselves were ready for the scrap heap.

The now aged employees looked at each other and said, "We have waited for no purpose, for after all our pensions are a load of crap."

A vice president of Human Resources overheard their lamentations in an area populated by company people of all ages, many young and impressionable, and immediately received authorization to terminate the geezers, with full retirement packages, of course (at current levels).

And since the Employee Recognition Program had been phased out in the late 1990s, nobody got a watch, either.

MORAL: PENSION SCHMENSION.

Mini-Fable

THE MICE VS. MCKINSEY, ROUND 2

The Mice had a staff meeting to decide how they might best devise means of warning themselves of the approach of their great enemy, the Consultant. Among the many plans suggested, the one that found most favor was the proposal to require anyone with an MBA from Wharton to check in with the front security desk before arriving in their midst. In this way, the Mice, being warned by a call from downstairs, might run away and hide themselves in remote cubicles at his approach. But when the Mice further debated who among them should call Human Resources to suggest this policy, there was no one found to do it, so it never happened, and all but the least expensive of them, a mouse named Mort, was laid off on the night before Christmas.

MORAL: THE WEAK MAY INHERIT THE EARTH,
BUT THEY DO VERY POORLY IN THE WORKPLACE.

The Chairman's Assistant appeared at the door and said,
"Edgar decided it was more important for him to go
to Davos. You'll have to get him out of this."

And Now

an Important Word About Priorities

|||||||||||||||||||||||||||||||

A Gigantic Project emerged at the end of the third quarter—
a presentation to a group of hungry bankers at an industry
boondoggle in Las Vegas. The cries and screams of those who
bore the weight of preparing for this Gigantic Project could
be heard for miles and miles surrounding the corporate headquarters for months on end. The lights burned throughout
the endless night, as pale, trembling Morlocks tried to grind
the statistics into digestible form again and again for the im-
perious and increasingly nervous Chairman. As the days until
the completion and delivery of the Gigantic Project dwin-
dled, the entire building became even more agitated. Loud
moaning from the basement and other assorted noises were
heard, and crowds of people came from all floors to the central hub of the operation so that they might discern the cause
of the racket.

The night before they were all to leave for Vegas, as they
assembled for a final run-through of the Gigantic Project, the

Chairman's Assistant appeared at the door and said, "Edgar decided it was more important for him to go to Davos. You'll have to get him out of this."

MORAL: THINGS ARE OFTEN MUCH LESS CRUCIAL THAN THEY MAY APPEAR AT THE TIME.

Mini-Fable
THREE CONVENIENT SOLUTIONS

A great and nefarious banking institution found itself attacked by just about everybody—regulators, the media, its customers. In fact, nobody liked them and many wanted them destroyed entirely, for good reasons that need not be explained. A big meeting at an expensive resort was convened to address this critical problem. The General Counsel of the enterprise offered an earnest presentation outlining how a spirited legal strategy would offer the best resistance. The Public Relations officer, for his part, strongly recommended an enhanced and very expensive media campaign. The Chief Financial Officer then gave an impassioned speech recommending an aggressive and immediate mix of increased dividends, a massive share buyback, and a tremendous and costly acquisition that would confuse everybody and distract them from all prior concerns.

MORAL: EVERYBODY WANTS TO THINK OUTSIDE THE BOX UNLESS IT'S THEIR BOX.

The Management Consultant, who had graduated with honors
from some business school or other, approached the Chief
Operating Officer in private and volunteered to be his spy.

Politics

Makes Smart

Bedfellows

||||||||||||||||||||||||||||

The head of Human Resources and a Management Consultant hired by the Chairman entered into an open-ended association for their mutual protection and benefit. Having done so, they went out into the field to hunt for pelts. The two had procceded only as far as their Cincinnati IT center when they ran into Bud, their Chief Operating Officer, who was doing a tour of line operations, looking primarily for areas of potential growth, since he was convinced that all the fat had now been excised and that any further reengineering would take out muscle and bone.

For this reason, matters were not cordial between the Chief Operating Officer and the Human Resources Executive, each of whom found themselves on the opposite end of their Chairman's confusing plateful of corporate agendas.

Perceiving a certain coolness between the powerful COO and the staff guy who was paying his fee, the Management Consultant, who had graduated with honors from some business school or other, approached the Chief Operating Officer in private and volunteered to be his spy. If the ultra-senior officer would pledge to extend his contract when the time came for the next corporate reorganization, then the Consultant would deliver a variety of tasty, confidential facts about the Human Resources Executive to the Chief Operating Officer. Then the Human Resources executive would be dead meat.

The Chief Operating Officer could see no downside in this. So, upon receiving appropriate assurances, the Management Consultant led his ostensible friend the HR Guy to a deep pit and arranged that he should fall into it.

The night before the dreaded deed was to be done, the COO called the HR Guy at home. It is very disquieting to receive a call like that at home, as anybody who has ever gotten one can tell you. "Carter," said the COO. "Your boy is about to sell you out. He's a real weasel, you know. Why do you have him around?"

"To keep an eye on him," said the HR Guy. "I guess I'm not doing a very good job."

"Carter," said the COO. "You're being a real pain in the ass to me about a whole bunch of things and you've thoroughly pissed me off for years, really. This whole thing would fuck you royally, and maybe that's not so bad."

At this point, the HR Guy, at home in his boxer shorts, sat down on the floor and leaned against the wall, as if he had been knocked over.

"But I don't think I'm going to need to worry about that shit from you anymore, am I?"

"No, sir," said Carter. "You're not."

Carter wondered what he would do about his loyalty to Jack, the CEO, his friend and mentor, who worried constantly about the ascendance of Bud and all his Budness. "I will have to deal with that later," said the HR Guy to himself after the conversation, while he was drinking a water glass filled to the brim with gin.

With Carter in Human Resources now well in hand, the Chief Operating Office then turned on the Management Consultant and ate his contract, ejecting him from the corporate body forever.

In the end, you will be happy to know that Carter worked out his loyalty issues. It was relatively easy after Jack announced his retirement. This was around the same time Carter's own employment contract came up for review, at which point it was firmly established that Bud was the dog and Carter was the tail. The two were friends ever afterward.

MORAL: THEY DON'T TEACH YOU EVERYTHING AT BUSINESS SCHOOL.

There was a fight, and the police were called, and each and
every one of them was hauled off to the hoosegow.

The Silly

Salesmen Laid Low
by the
Sexy Strippers
and Their Own
Stupidity

||||||||||||||||||||||||||

A number of Salesmen visited a Gentlemen's Club at the edge of a town where they were attending a convention and, settling themselves in there until the small hours of the morning, enjoyed themselves in a manner not consistent with corporate guidelines.

By the wee hours, they had lost all sense of propriety and control, and were so incredibly wasted they could not tell their butts from a hole in the ground. At one point or another, several found themselves brimming with excessive sentiment and became amorous with the dancers, which brought the bouncers, and there was a fight, and the police were called, and each and every one of them was hauled off to the hoosegow.

The next morning, unable to appear at their booth on the convention floor to sell their wares to impressionable visitors from Asia, they were all fired by the President of Worldwide Sales, who was utterly infuriated at having to man the booth and pitch the product himself. As they sat in jail, unemployed and soon to be divorced, they decried their fate, exclaiming, "O foolish creatures that we are, for the sake of a little pleasure we have destroyed ourselves!"

MORAL: ONLY YOU CAN PREVENT FOREST FIRES.

Mini-Fable

NO FLIES ON THE CORPORATE GUYS

One year, the global economy got freaked out by one nation or another's financial collapse and went into a tailspin that sucked everybody down for a couple of years. During this storm, the President of a large firm that sold interstitial widgets had to make some tough decisions. First he got rid of his Public Relations people, because that was easy. Then he tossed his Marketing guys overboard, because they were expensive and he couldn't afford their recommendations anyway. The recession still continuing, he finally called a meeting of his very senior staff. "Guys," he said, "we have a choice. We can start cutting Sales, which produces revenue, or we can really tighten our belts around here—cut our own expenses, fire the executive chef, sell the plane, that kind of stuff. What do you say?" The corporate guys thought about it for a moment, then said, "Cut Sales, definitely."

MORAL: THERE'S A REASON CERTAIN PEOPLE MAKE IT TO THE TOP.

The CEO called the offending group into his 3,000-square-foot office and screamed at them like an insane child for more than two hours.

The
Potentially
Generous CEO and
the Idiots Who
Misjudged the Depths
of His Largesse

|||||||||||||||||||||||||||||||||

Aworld-class battleship of a CEO who led a powerful multinational corporation was conducting an Off-Site for his group of fifty top managers. Together, their clothing and accessories alone were worth more than 2 million euros.

The theme of the event centered around "Exponential Growth in the Time of Cholera," a literary reference hit upon by the CEO himself, who viewed himself as an intellectual as well as a great businessperson.

The site of the boondoggle was the home of their West Coast office, San Francisco, a city perfectly positioned near a small forest of dot-coms that would make juicy eating.

During the course of the three-day meeting, which took place over a weekend so that no weekday time should be lost, the CEO spotted one of the finer restaurants in a town known for them. Somewhat tired of the food at the Four Seasons Hotel, where their meeting was being held, and as a gesture of generosity toward his senior staff, he booked a large table at the restaurant close to the Embarcadero that featured not only four-star cuisine but lovely, warm ambience and a lively crowd.

Right before dinner, however, the CEO ran into a potential customer at the hotel bar, the young President of an Internet start-up who was drunk and in an expository mood. Smelling an even bigger dinner than the one he had arranged for his staff, the CEO bailed on his own but urged his posse to go on ahead and enjoy themselves anyhow.

The group, after certain feeble protestations, duly went, and thoroughly entranced with the place, proceeded to order foie gras, steaks, lobsters, stuff with rare truffles in it, and soufflés, each course accompanied by a raft of very special wines suggested by the sommelier, including one storied Bordeaux that ran $1,200 per bottle, which the oenophile in the group declared "a bargain at that price." The merry band, having already consumed several cocktails and about a gallon of *vin* slightly more *ordinaire* each, ordered not one but two bottles of the remarkable nectar.

Back in Chicago, the CEO was presented with the bill by his outraged Controller, who had not been invited to the gathering because he was not much fun at such events. Equally enraged, the CEO called the offending group into his 3,000-square-foot office and shook the bill in their faces and screamed at them like an insane child for more than two hours. At one point, his gums reportedly began to bleed, so high was his blood pressure and the brute force of his yelling. Then he made them pay for it personally.

The following January, he stiffed them on their bonuses, too.

MORAL: IF YOU'RE GOING TO ORDER A $1,200 BOTTLE OF WINE, MAKE SURE IT'S CHARGED TO A CLIENT.

Two years later, the former Junior Vice President
cashed in his equity for $800 million.

The Veep

and the

Creep

||||||||||||||||||||||||||||

A Junior Vice President of somewhat tender years ran into a senior Finance guy in the employee cafeteria, where the younger had come to eat and the elder was making sure the stale bread from yesterday was being reused. The corporation spent more than $285,000 on supplies per year in the employee cafeteria, and the senior guy, who was also in charge of Corporate Compensation, was concerned about that.

Seizing this rare opportunity to consult with the more powerful officer, the Junior Vice President begged him for a small stipend from the Company's bonus pool that year, since he was in good standing with his bosses and many at his level were so graced. "Sure," said the Compensation Officer, keeping his eye on a slice of bologna that had fallen on the floor but was still perfectly good. "Possibly next year. This year is looking a little lean."

Noticing the disappointment (along with some mustard) on the fellow's face, he added, "And if you hang in there for another two or three years, we'll take a look at getting you into the stock option plan as well."

The Junior Vice President heartily thanked the Compensation Officer, then went back to his cubicle and put his résumé into play. Six weeks later, he was offered a slot at a much smaller place that gave him a bit of equity. When he announced his departure, the Compensation Officer, who hated losing young and talented people who consented to be underpaid, asked him why he was going.

"I'm very grateful for all you've done for me, Pip," said the Junior Vice President. The guy's name really was Pip. "But I can't think that if you choke on a 10 percent bonus now, you'll at some point in the future do anything really significant on my behalf."

Two years later, the former Junior Vice President cashed in his equity for $800 million. He now lives on a 10,000-acre ranch in Wyoming.

And the Compensation Officer was still getting by on six hundred grand a year.

MORAL: PEOPLE WITH NO HISTORY OF GENEROSITY RARELY DEVELOP ANY LATER IN LIFE.

Mini-Fable

THE LIMITS OF THINKING AT 35,000 FEET

A Strategic Planning person was flying back to Northern California on American Airlines, in the first-class cabin, which is a lot less special than it sounds but is still better than a sharp stick in the eye. After two double Glenlivets, he fell to musing over the plan he was perfecting on his laptop. "The money we'll generate from this strategy will generate at least half a dozen new development efforts. Those will most certainly produce one actual application that can be monetized across a wide range of platforms. If we move swiftly, the whole deal will be ready by Christmas, when it will fetch the highest price, generating significant revenue this year and pumping my annual bonus through the moon! Yes!" So excited was he by this fantasy that he actually pumped his fist in triumph, inadvertently hit the wrong key on the laptop, and erased his entire presentation, which he had failed to back up due to a faulty belief in his own invincibility.

MORAL: STRATEGIC PLANNING MAY BE AN OVERRATED DISCIPLINE, AT LEAST IN THIS WORLD.

The President of Sales descended on the department with a rigorous
zero-based reorganization and defenestrated a great number.

The President

of Sales

vs.

the Lazy

Sales Weasels

||||||||||||||||||||||||||||

Some Lazy Sales Weasels had become accustomed to hanging around their department day after day, doing pretty much nothing except going to lunch with putative clients, drinking coffee from their new, pretentious Nespresso machine, and otherwise feeding off the capacious nipple of the corporation without generating squat in the way of incoming revenue.

For a long time the President of Sales, brandishing nothing more than a bunch of empty exhortations and threats, could get them up off their butts for a couple of hours at a time, succeeding mostly in driving them across the street to the local pub.

When the Lazy Sales Weasels found that the President of their division was mostly slinging nothing but hot air, however, they didn't even do that, remaining inert and uninspired for days at a time, laughing and scratching, and essentially waiting for the two or three weeks in early June when the industry went nuts and orders came in almost by themselves.

The President of Sales, on seeing this general level of indolence and insolence, descended on the department with a rigorous zero-based reorganization motored by a truly vicious consultant, and defenestrated a great number, casting them out into the world, where many were forced to get jobs selling Internet banner inventory or other gigs even more humiliating. The surviving weasels, scared out of their tiny minds, at once hit the streets with their most serious briefcases, crying to each other, "It is time for us to be off to Madison Avenue, Silicon Valley, and Detroit, for our boss is no longer content to scare us, but begins to show us in earnest what he can do."

MORAL: IF WORDS SUFFICE NOT, BLOWS MUST FOLLOW.

The Reporter came up and prodded, poked, and smelled
him all over, while the terrified Mogul held his breath and feigned
the appearance of total vacuity as much as he could.

The Reporter

from a
Leading Financial
Publication
and the
Two Priapic Moguls

|||||||||||||||||||||||||||||

Two Priapic Moguls were attending the World Economic Forum in Davos when a Reporter from a leading financial publication accosted them on the jogging path. One of them climbed up quickly into a tree and concealed himself in the branches. The other, seeing no other recourse, fell flat on the ground and feigned a small stroke that rendered him inert, and when the Reporter came up and prodded, poked, and smelled him all over, the terrified Mogul held his breath and feigned the appearance of total vacuity as much as he could.

The Reporter stood there for a time quite silently, then murmured a few words in the Mogul's tiny ear and departed. In general a journalist will not touch a source that it believes is already dead.

When he was quite gone, the other Mogul descended from the tree, and jocularly inquired of his friend what it was the Reporter had whispered in his ear. His companion replied,

"He told me, 'With friends like Lenny up in that big tree there, you don't need enemies.'"

MORAL: A FRIEND IN NEED IS HARD TO FIND DURING A TWENTY-FOUR-HOUR NEWS CYCLE.

Mini-Fable

THE SURVIVAL OF THE QUISLINGS

On his way out the door, a truly smart, accomplished, and decent executive ran into a bunch of quislings who were coming back from a late lunch that had begun rather early. "I don't get it," said the disappointed former boss, who hadn't seen the ax coming. "I wonder how you guys, who are total lightweights, manage to survive while so many better men and women have gone in and out of this place." After a moment of reflection, one of the quislings, it doesn't really matter which, replied, "Guys like you don't know how to bend. That's all we know how to do. We survive because we're lightweights, not in spite of it."

MORAL: YOU'VE GOT TO PLAY THE GAME THAT GOT YOU HERE.

They each entered the building at precisely 8:52 a.m. every day, and waited for the same elevator, each with a newspaper and a cup of coffee. That was where all similarities ended.

When
Worlds Collide

||||||||||||||||||||||||||||||

A young woman condemned to a middling position in the Internal Communications Department of an advertising agency saw a Haute Executive of Uncertain Portfolio in the lobby of her building every morning as he arrived at work. He didn't know what she did. She didn't know what he did. They each entered the building at precisely 8:52 a.m. every day, and waited for the same elevator, each with a newspaper and a cup of coffee. That was where all similarities ended. The young woman got off on the third floor, where she repaired to a small office with no windows. The Haute Executive of Uncertain Portfolio rose to the fifty-second floor, where he occupied approximately eight hundred square feet of space overlooking the river, with a panoramic view of the city and several states beyond.

"You know what?" said the young woman to herself one day. "I bet if I looked like that guy I would do a whole lot better than I'm doing right now." This she proceeded to do, acquiring six or seven fine suits with the greater part of her savings, and frequenting several of the restaurants and watering holes favored by the Haute Executive.

Unlike her wealthier counterpart, who was long practiced in the pampered executive life, the young woman marooned in Internal Communications was unfamiliar with the fare in these dining establishments and always left them hungry and virtually penniless. She continued with her campaign, however, to the point where she would exclaim, "Délicieux!" upon finishing a three-ounce portion of foie gras on a toast point the size of a postage stamp. Then she'd go home and eat a gallon of ice cream.

After six months of this lifestyle, she had expended her allotted corporate credit limit and had ballooned to nearly 180 pounds. Her career was in shambles.

One day, while plodding around the reservoir in Central Park attempting to shed her third tire, she was mugged for her watch. It was a knockoff. Surviving this episode, she suddenly saw the error of her materialistic ways, quit corporate life altogether, moved to San Francisco, and became a shaman, preaching the simple life of the soul and oneness with all that lives and breathes in maya.

Today, she has several best-selling books under a spiritual imprint and owns two Mercedeses and a Maybach.

MORAL: YOU CAN GET WITH THIS. OR YOU CAN GET WITH THAT.

Mini-Fable

THE FILM COMPANY NOBODY WANTED

Once upon a time, there was a film company that had essentially been run into the ground and was nothing more than a lame library and a couple of limp producers with expensive deals that would never earn back. Nevertheless, the worldwide hunger for content being what it is, two respectable entertainment companies vied for possession of the enterprise. Each did its due diligence, lined up potential financing, and spent hours and hours looking at some way the property could justify the cost associated with its acquisition. After months of this, both organizations were totally and utterly exhausted by the exercise, and still neither could make the numbers work. During a lapse in the proceedings, along came a hedge fund with a bunch of stupid money from the Middle East and, over the course of one long weekend, it snapped up the target company, which in the end brought nothing but aggravation to the victors.

MORAL: WINNERS OF A LOSER ARE LOSERS, AND THE LOSERS, WINNERS.

The Miserly Mogul found the safe room empty and
began to tear at his sparse hair and howl.

The
Miserable

Miserly Mogul
Gets Served

|||||||||||||||||||||||||||

The Miserable Miserly Mogul sold all of the cash, stocks, and other instruments of wealth that he had accumulated over a lifetime and bought a large suitcase full of bearer bonds, which he proceeded to put in a safe room in the basement of his opulent, walled-in castle in Beverly Hills. Each day, he would repair to the room, which was secured with several magnetic locks of intricate design, and gaze at his stash with a love that would have been unseemly if it weren't so sad.

"Ah, my beauties," he would murmur to himself, petting the stacks of paper with a trembling hand. "The financial instruments of this world may come and go, but there will always be you."

Although he was a Miserable Miserly Mogul, he still did require many workmen to sustain his ostensibly frugal lifestyle, including gardeners, cooks, housekeepers, security people, even a man whose job it was to feed his tropical birds, which although able to speak uttered nothing but expletives. One of these laborers was a clever and observant individual whose duty was to make sure the pH of the swimming pool was precisely calibrated.

One day, while scooping out leaves from the massive body of chlorinated water, this fellow noticed his employer furtively looking around, then disappearing into the bowels of the house. The pool man followed, and witnessed the process by which the Miserly Mogul gained entry to his secret room. That very night, the greedy young fellow slipped into the house, for which he had keys. He went down into the basement and, without too much trouble, unlocked the safe room where the glorious, completely negotiable hoard was housed. "Yikes," he said.

He then placed it carefully in a capacious backpack he had brought exactly for the purpose, quietly put it in the trunk of his car, and headed for the Dalmatian Coast of Croatia, rumored to be a lovely area where one's money goes a lot further than at other resorts of its nature, and quite pleasant now that they seem to be done with all that ethnic cleansing.

The Miserly Mogul, on his next visit, found the safe room empty and began to tear at his sparse hair and howl so loud that he was heard by one of his celebrity neighbors, who drove a golf cart over and, seeing him overcome with grief and learning the cause, said, "Chill out, Bernard. Go get a big stone from your koi pond and lug it to your super-secure little room and imagine that your big large suitcase full of bearer bonds is still there. It will do you just about as much good. You did nothing with the things while you had them anyhow."

MORAL: USE IT OR LOSE IT.

"Hey, where are you, Brewster?" said the Chairman.
"I need some company."

The
Unquestionably Sick
(but Still
Quite Dangerous)
Chairman

||||||||||||||||||||||||||||||

A Chairman, unable because of old age and myriad infirmities to provide himself with sufficient compensation to sustain his lifestyle, in spite of the fact that it already numbered in the tens of millions of dollars, resolved to cadge some extra lucre by artifice. He retired to his den and, lying down there, pretended to be sick, taking care that his sickness be publicly known.

His fellow senior officers, who were jostling for positional benefit upon his demise, expressed their sorrow, and came one by one to his den, where the Chairman devoured them, stealing their stock options, questioning their expense accounts and their use of the corporate jet, and so forth.

After many of the beasts had thus disappeared into the corporate ether, a junior vice president in the Strategic Planning Department discerned how the ostensibly ailing Chairman was cleverly swallowing most of high middle management.

So one day he called the Chairman on the telephone while the great beast was on the West Coast and he was on the East, and asked him how he was. "Very middling," replied the halting voice on the other end of the line, "but, hey, where are you, Brewster?

202 | STANLEY BING

Hop on the G4 and we can talk about it. I need some company."

"No, thank you," said the young executive. "I notice that there are many prints of feet entering that den of yours, but no trace of any returning."

MORAL: HE IS WISE WHO IS WARNED BY THE MISFORTUNES OF OTHERS.

Mini-Fable

TRANSITION THIS, BABE

A Senior Officer got wind that his corporation was going to be acquired by a competitor. Upon receiving this disquieting news, he went to see his pal, a lower-middle-management grunt in the Public Relations Department of the company. "We should put our résumés in play," said the Senior Officer. "I know a few headhunters who can help us." "Oh, I don't know," said his friend. "Let me ask you something. You think the new guys are going to need somebody to work with their guys on the press releases, deal with the media, handle the press conference, that kind of thing?" "Well, yeah," said the Senior Officer. "Good," said the PR guy. "Then I'll take my chance with the new guys. You, on the other hand, are toast, my friend." "Tell me something I don't know," said the Senior Officer, and took the buyout.

MORAL: THE NEW BOSS IS THE SAME AS THE OLD BOSS UNLESS *YOU* USED TO BE THE OLD BOSS. IN THAT CASE, THERE'S A BIG DIFFERENCE.

He was so resentful that his mind couldn't focus for even one tiny little moment on his own failures of leadership and comportment. And in this lack of self-examination and insight there was tremendous strength.

The Former
CEO
Who Would Be
King

||||||||||||||||||||||||||||

A CEO was ejected from his post as the head of a corporation by its Board of Directors, which felt he had done a very lousy job. "These are some very disloyal Directors," said the CEO on his way out the door. "I put them in their places, gave them nice compensation for serving at my every whim, and now look at what they've done to me." He was so resentful that his mind couldn't focus for even one tiny little moment on his own failures of leadership and comportment. And in this lack of self-examination and insight there was tremendous strength that powered this executive to look for the next big opportunity in the grandiose saga that was the legend in his own mind.

And so it was that a group of badgers, stoats, and ferrets found where he had gone to ground, and approached him with a proposition. "You were such an excellent CEO," said the head badger to his former majesty, "that it occurs to us that you might like to be a King."

"Really," said the former CEO. "Tell me more."

"Well," said a rather well-heeled stoat, who was the

best-spoken among the representatives. "You have all the skills. You are charming when in public. You are personable when called upon to be so. You can sit in meetings whose length and content are established beforehand by you. You can represent the interests of your friends while supposedly talking about the public weal, since pretending you care about stockholders is very much like pretending to care about the public."

At this, the former CEO laughed. And then so did they all.

"And you have a great deal of money," concluded the stoat.

"Money?" asked the former CEO, who liked his money and was loath to part with it.

"Oh, yes," said the vole in charge of fiduciary matters. "A King must spend a lot of money, first to get into the castle and then to remain there. In olden days, the public paid for a position of such importance. But nowadays that piddling amount does not suffice and most who succeed to even a small Kingship are at least partially self-funded. That should be no problem for you, though. You're loaded."

"Indeed," said the former CEO, who was now quite interested. The future lay before him, boring and uneventful, for he knew it was highly unlikely that any other Board of Directors would select him to do anything interesting.

"I'll do it," said the former CEO.

And so it was that this extremely mediocre business executive bought his way into a very nice Kingship in a pleasant wine-producing region of the realm. And he reigned for several years, representing very assiduously those who had helped him achieve his elevated status, and pretty much ignoring everybody else, which was, after all, what he had been trained for.

MORAL: WHEN COMMON SENSE AND REASON FAIL, SUCCESS WILL SURELY FOLLOW.

He felt momentarily ashamed, as he had never been before,
of their tatty little coffee room and their common kitchen area,
which smelled of bean sprouts and spirulina.

The City
Mouse
and the
Country Mouse

||||||||||||||||||||||||||||||

Once upon a time, there was a high-powered executive who ate raw glass for breakfast, and he worked sixteen hours a day in a steel tower in the dead center of the biggest city in the world. One day, this captain of industry was called upon to visit his counterpart in another corporation that operated out of a softer region of the country, a place where food and wine make the front page of the daily newspaper and people put soy in their coffee.

The captain of industry looked about him at his friend's headquarters. There were no offices, per se. People had cubicles and areas they occupied when they felt the need. All space was wide open, and the conference rooms had cute little names, like "Borsalino" and "Hopscotch," so that when someone had a meeting, they might say, "I'm going to play Hopscotch now," and everybody would know where they were going for a while. Workers arrived and left when they wished. There was a kitchen filled with healthy food and drink. Everybody called each other by their first names and wore blue jeans, including the President. Lunch, that nexus of business power in the big city, was here taken in common areas, or grabbed at one's desk.

"Chuck," said the powerful business nabob to his younger, hipper friend, "I'm here to offer you a job. I can see how pleasant it is around here, but really, where are you going with it? Come to New York. Be my number two. I'll pay you a bundle, with a good chunk of equity. You're twiddling your thumbs here. Play in the big game. You're ready."

The young executive thought about it. Suddenly the office around him looked sort of rinky-dink. The forced informality of it all appeared threadbare and like something of an affectation. He felt momentarily ashamed, as he had never been before, of their tatty little coffee room and their common kitchen area, which smelled of bean sprouts and spirulina.

"Okay, Bob," he said to the older executive. "I'll do it."

Six weeks later, Chuck was ensconced in his office on the sixty-seventh floor of a tower in downtown Manhattan. That day, he had a muffin behind his closed door, by himself. Then he had large, structured financial reviews of various operating divisions of the corporation that ran from 8:00 to 10:00 a.m. and 10:15 to 12:45, a working lunch with the executive team between 1:00 p.m. and 2:30, and then meetings with employees who were eager to get to know their new boss until about 7:00 p.m. He then went home to his new apartment in a humongous residential tower, drank a bunch of scotch, and fell asleep.

This routine was, to one degree or another, repeated for the next several years, during which time his marriage dissolved, his children dropped out of college, and he developed a horrible case of eczema. Every now and then he would visit the big kahuna who had hired him and comment on the misery of their mutual existence.

"Why do we do it this way, Bob?" he asked the older, presumably wiser executive.

"Because it's fun!" said the prince of the city. And he meant it, too.

Finally, able to take it no longer, the no-longer-quite-young Mouse abruptly quit the corporate life and ran back to the coast from whence he had come. There he assumed a perfectly appropriate management position in a small, thriving little operation that needed a person of his experience, wisdom, and charm. Not long after, he was found at his desk in an advanced stage of rigor mortis, facedown in the remains of his daily healthy luncheon salad.

The coroner's report concluded that he had died of boredom.

MORAL: YOU CAN'T GO HOME AGAIN. TRY TO FIND A NICE HOTEL INSTEAD.

Final
Note

||||||||||||||||||||||||||||||

I'd like to take a moment to thank Aesop for all the good stories and characters he laid down on his way to being stoned to death by his last humorless audience.

When I was thinking about this little book, I read through hundreds and hundreds of his fables. Sometimes it was tough to see what he was thinking about, or who he was making fun of with all those frogs and beavers and ravens, and sometimes rather inscrutable little morals. But after a while, as I made my way through them, it became clear to me that many of the lessons contained within were extremely germane not so much in everyday life but most certainly in the world of business, where foxes, wolves, lions, bears, and weasels still run free.

I hope that in this effort I have been true to the intent and spirit of the original, and that, where I have not, I have at least bent and masticated it with appropriate reverence and purpose.

—STANLEY BING